The Happy Lawyer Handbook

Mitchell Nathanson

CONTENTS

3

Introduction

So, you've decided to become a lawyer. Congratulations. Unfortunately, most people construe these congratulations as evidence that their career choice has now been made and they can, therefore, move on to their next life obstacle. These people eventually make up the thousands of unhappy lawyers who populate law firms, corporations and many other professional walks of life. Because you have this book in your hands, you will not become one of these people. So, once again, congratulations.

The truth is that the decision to become a lawyer is not really a decision at all. Rather, it is a step, albeit a major (not to mention expensive) one, along a path that requires you to think deeply, research carefully and plan meticulously if you hope to end up among the few, the proud, the *happy* lawyers who likewise populate law firms, corporations and many other professional walks of life. Contrary to much of the chatter heard about lawyers (most of which comes from lawyers themselves), it is not only possible, it is relatively easy to develop and maintain a career in the law that is not only financially, but emotionally satisfying, regardless of the state of the overall economy. The trick is to understand the nature of the legal employment market and your place in it, not only today but down the road as well. Armed with this knowledge, you will be able to avoid the pitfalls that so often engulf young lawyers and send them careening into a negative career spiral that causes them to spend their entire professional lives working for people they do not like and on issues in which they have no interest. You will be equipped to manage the market such that you will be able to develop a career that feeds your passion and avoid a succession of jobs that do not. *The Happy Lawyer Handbook* will guide you through this process.

In order to fully understand what it takes to be satisfied, however, it is first necessary to understand just why it is that so many lawyers are frustrated. Because, rest assured, the unhappy lawyers you hear about in the media or at your dinner table did not set out to be unhappy. They were once in your shoes and, like you, envisioned a career that fulfilled them emotionally, not merely financially. If asked, most of them probably would not be able to pinpoint the moment things went wrong for them. Instead, they would most likely mention things such as bosses, deadlines or clients as the cause of their misery. But these things exist in many different professions; professions which have, overall, much greater job satisfaction rates than does the practice of law. Deadlines exist, no matter what your profession, as do irritating clients and overbearing bosses. So it must be something else. And it is. Perhaps it would surprise you (it would surely surprise them) to learn that the cause of attorney despair is very often rooted in factors that play out long before you even meet your boss, miss a deadline or sign your first client. Because, as it turns out, the blueprint for misery is drawn while you're still in law school. And it is often completed without your knowledge. How is this possible? Consider the following:

As a law student, you're concerned with much more than torts and contracts and constitutional law. While these things are nice, you'd also like

5

a job after graduation as well. After all, if you're like most people, you did not go to law school merely for the academic exercise. Conveniently for you, there is a career services office located in the building which focuses on nothing else. So you, like almost everyone else in your class, utilize it, more or less, most likely by availing yourself of the school's local law firm database and perhaps, if your grades merit it, its on-campus law firm recruitment activities, and perhaps by signing up for interviews during the fall of your second year. You've based your selection of firms (or corporations or government entities) on their reputation (word travels fast within legal circles), size and probably salary (word travels even faster with regard to this). You've also probably paged through your copy of the National Association for Law Placement (NALP) directory to get some idea of the range of practice areas within particular firms, although as a law student, you probably do not know exactly what attorneys in law firms do every day, nor do you even know what "Insurance Coverage Litigation" means, except that 40% of the lawyers in your top choice firm practice in this area.

Oh well, you tell yourself, you'll figure that part out later, after you've spent some time there if you're lucky enough to get an offer. What's more important is that the firm is known for its collegial environment and, more to the point, the starting salary is more than your father ever made in his life. What's the worst that can happen? you ask yourself. If you don't like it, you can always go somewhere else later. And if, after discovering what insurance coverage litigation is, you decide that you don't like that either, you can always shift your area of practice later as well. You can't possibly go wrong at a firm like this, you tell yourself. Unfortunately, you already have. To such a degree that you will most likely be unable to undo your mistakes for years, if ever.

Tragically, and without your even realizing it, you have already started down a path of employment that will very likely cause you years of misery because, much as you suspected, you do not like insurance coverage litigation, only now it's too late to do anything about it. Although you did not realize it at the time, the job you selected out of law school has indelibly branded you and limited your ability to switch practice areas (even within your firm) now that you have some experience under your belt. In the eyes of the legal world (both within your firm and without), an insurance coverage lawyer is what you are and what you will be, your protestations to the contrary. And you do protest. At the dinner table and, if given the opportunity, in the media, railing about deadlines, irritating clients and overbearing bosses. But as this all too familiar scenario has shown, they have nothing to do with your unhappiness. The seeds, so to speak, were sown back while you were still in law school. Stealthily planted while you thought you were doing all you could do to ensure professional happiness. Because of your failure to understand how the legal employment market operates while you were in law school, you naively accepted a generic "job" upon graduation rather than making an informed career decision. And now that job has become your career as that decision has been made for you, whether you like it or not. And by this point, there's not much you can do about it.

Of course, there's something you can do about it now. And that's where *The Happy Lawyer Handbook* comes in. It is said that knowledge is power and as a reader of this book, you will understand the roots of professional dissatisfaction and, armed with this knowledge, will be able to conduct a thoughtful career search that focuses on your long term goals and interests rather than merely attempting to wrangle yourself into the first, or highest paying, job available. You will understand the hiring process not merely as it pertains to newly-minted grads such as yourself but how it subtly changes as you gain experience, and will therefore avoid being pigeonholed for the rest of your career in an unfulfilling area of law; you will learn how to identify your passions and how to ensure that the area of law in which you practice is personally satisfying and not merely a dreary (and ultimately frustrating) means to a paycheck. In short, you will know what you are getting into before you get into it. Because you don't want to be that guy on television or at the dinner table. And you don't have to be. For as you'll learn by the end of this book, perhaps it should also be said that knowledge brings happiness. So congratulations on your decision to become a lawyer. Now it's time to get started on the really important stuff.

Chapter One: Happiness and the Legal Culture

Of course, everyone wants to be happy. However, as a law student or young lawyer, you have probably come across dozens of lawyers who discuss professional happiness as a lofty, somewhat unreachable goal. Something that, while important *someday*, must necessarily give way to other, more pressing concerns. In the eyes of many law students and young attorneys, happiness simply isn't something that can be reasonably attained right out of the chute. Unfortunately, it is this mindset that sends them off into a career spiral that eventually renders professional happiness unattainable forever.

Happiness Leads to Success Rather than Follows It

Typically, young lawyers make one of two conceptual mistakes: either they equate their level of success with their expected level of happiness or they believe that happiness is a byproduct of success. Often, the same person makes both mistakes at different stages of their career. For instance, they may initially believe that happiness cannot even be considered a reasonable goal at this embryonic stage of their career because they believe that since it naturally takes years to build a successful practice, it must likewise take years to develop professional satisfaction. Built into this framework, however, is the assumption that as the years pass and as they rise

9

through their firm's hierarchy from first year associate to second year to third year and so on, job satisfaction will likewise incrementally increase on its own without any input on their part. Of course, as the years go by and happiness does not increase as expected, the young lawyer then begins to realize that perhaps his or her initial assumption that the level of success dictates the level of happiness may have been incorrect. However, rather than reevaluate their mindset, many young lawyers subtly shift their assumptions to accommodate their perpetual discontent.

It is at this point that they then begin to believe that perhaps happiness *in any form* does not come until complete and total success is achieved. Therefore, they reassure themselves that their present unhappiness represents nothing more than a necessary period of "dues-paying" which will eventually pay off in a big way, emotionally as well as financially. If only they can hold out until they make partner, they tell themselves, they will achieve professional Nirvana. This internal rationalization typically enables many young attorneys to navigate through the next several years of hard work and long hours where they spend most of their free time, as well as, unfortunately, most of their working time, daydreaming of all the things they'd rather be doing. In the end, of course, most young attorneys fail to make partner and either leave their firm or, worse, stay, transitioning into a non-partner-track position where they then are asked to perform much of the same thankless grunt work they had performed earlier, only now without the carrot of future partnership dangled before their eyes to motivate them.

Perhaps surprisingly, although they have never experienced happiness in the workplace, most disgruntled attorneys nevertheless fail to make the causal connection between their misery and their ultimate failure to achieve their professional goals. Rather, they oftentimes view their perpetual gloom as just desserts for failing to achieve their desired status in the workplace. In their minds, things would have been quite different if only they had made partner. If only they'd made partner, many attorneys believe, they would have achieved emotional, as well as financial, satisfaction. Unfortunately, they have everything backwards. For as this chapter will discuss, if only they were happy when they were younger, they'd have been more likely to achieve partnership (or other professional goals) later on.

Simply stated, happiness is a precursor to success rather than a result of it. Those who brush off happiness as a professional consideration are doing so at great risk to the careers in which they have invested so heavily. In short, they are dooming themselves to failure. A quick glimpse into a typical day of a young attorney, regardless of his or her field, illustrates why this is the case.

A Day in the Life of the Young Attorney

Depending on the region in which you practice, your day will begin at some point between eight and ten AM. Some legal communities, such as Philadelphia's, typically start on the early side, with eager associates often arriving at work as early as seven in the morning. Others, such as New York's, generally kick into gear later, perhaps owing to the later nights worked in Manhattan (after all, it's not called "the city that never sleeps" for nothing).

Once settled in at your desk, your first task will be reviewing hard-copy correspondence, motions and briefs that have arrived since you departed the previous evening as well as the torrent of emails that have piled up since the last time you logged on to your work account. While there is typically a 20 or 30-day period allotted for response to most court documents, the motions lying in your in-bin may have taken a circuitous route to your office, stopping first in the mailroom, then at various partners' desks along the way. Consequently, it is not uncommon for some, if not most of the response period to have elapsed before the motion finally reaches the hands of the person responsible for replying to it--yours. Although you had planned to spend this morning continuing your research for the trial brief you've been working on for the past several days, you now must re-prioritize given the impending deadlines you're now facing with regard to those newly received motions. Accordingly, you decide to tackle that trial brief tomorrow as you log onto Westlaw to start on your new project.

A short while later you run into a senior associate who asks you if you have some time later in the week to talk about her upcoming trial. There are some last minute briefs and motions *in limine* she has to prepare and, given all of the good things said about you by a partner you worked with earlier in a case dealing with similar issues, the senior associate would very much like for you to work with her as well. Of course you accept and tell her you'll stop by as soon as you finish responding to the motions you're now working on. She leaves and you make a mental note of both the appointment as well as the fact that you'll have to push off the trial brief research until later in the week.

You continue to work on your response motions for the rest of the morning. Finally, you decide to break for lunch. You return to your office to check your email before heading out for a sandwich, and see that your boss has emailed you from the cellphone he never seems to be without and which tethers the two of you together days, nights and weekends, particularly when he's on trial. He informs you of an unexpected evidentiary issue that has arisen in the case he's now trying and asks you to research it and update him on the law before court reconvenes later this afternoon. You grab a quick bite before heading back to your desk where you clear aside the materials you had been working on with regard to this morning's motions in order to make room for the cases you're now reading in order to clarify the evidentiary issue. You find the relevant case law, hurry back to your office, dash off a quick memo which you email back to your boss and then once again attempt to tackle those motions. In the meantime, the afternoon mail has arrived, replete with more motions and briefs requiring your attention. You also notice a new case file sitting on your chair, with a yellow stickie attached from the firm's file assignment partner informing you that the case is yours and that you are to "please handle" it. You briefly rifle through the file, checking to see if anything needs to be filed within the next 24 hours. Thankfully, there isn't. The statute of limitations does not expire until the day after next so thus, you have a full 36 hours to investigate, draft and file the complaint. You make a note of this, put the file aside and, for the third time, attempt to resume your research on this morning's motions. At some point later that evening, you realize that you're not going to get to that trial brief until next week at the earliest.

Whew! By any measure, that is a busy day. And that's not even taking into account the numerous phone calls, impromptu conferences, and outside "life issues" (boyfriend, girlfriend, family, pet crises) that also impede upon a typical day. Multiply all of the above by 365 (because, thanks to the Internet, very few attorneys are able to leave the office behind even during the weekend) and it's easy to see that there is no shortage of work and stress in a young attorney's life. How you manage not only the workload but the stress that accompanies it will ultimately determine your success as an attorney. And it is impossible to successfully manage both of these variables over the long haul if you don't inherently enjoy what you do. While you may be able to survive for a period of time, you'll never thrive and, as the following section shows, will eventually fall behind those associates who do love their work. They will be the ones who will ultimately achieve the success you had planned for yourself while you, competitively disadvantaged from the start, will be doomed to spend the rest of your career frustrated in the levels of both your emotional satisfaction and professional achievement.

Happiness as a Competitive Advantage

By its very nature, the practice of law is a competitive profession. However, despite protestations to the contrary from law firms of all sizes, the competition is not limited to the courtroom. In order to survive, law firms must employ many more associates than they could possibly ever hope to promote to partnership. A quick glimpse through a National Association for Law Placement (NALP) directory shows that firms typically employ, at a minimum, two to three times as many associates as partners. While this may be a necessity so as to enable these firms to adequately handle the staggering amount of work required to properly maintain their voluminous caseloads, this also means that as a young associate, you are competing with your fellow associates for a limited number of partnership positions. Although many firms (particularly large ones) vehemently deny that such a competitive atmosphere exists within their confines, their associate/partner ratios necessarily dictates that the firm's culture be significantly less collegial than

14

they'd have you believe. As a result, although it is an unfortunate reality of law firm life, the associates sitting in the offices to your right and left will most likely be the largest impediments to your reaching your professional goals. Given this fact, it will naturally be the people who most capably handle the work and stresses of the job that advance. And those people will naturally be the people who love what they do.

Consider the typical workday described above. Because your firm employs 100 associates and 50 partners, now consider that you and a fellow associate in your employment discrimination litigation department are naturally competing for the one partnership position that will eventually become available to the two of you. Although you both want to succeed, your rival loves employment discrimination law while you were assigned to the department by the firm even though your real interest is in entertainment law. You enjoy the paycheck well enough but find employment discrimination law to be substantively very dry and overly technical. Your rival, however, reads employment contracts during her lunch hour and is putting together a manual of employment "do's and don'ts" for the firm's clients in her free time. While you leave work the moment your daily crisis has been resolved, she typically stays late into the evening, or takes work home with her, even when there is nothing pending the next day because she just enjoys reading through her case files to get a better grasp of the issues that confront her clients. It's not difficult to guess which of the two of you will eventually be asked to join the partnership.

As this example illustrates, it is virtually impossible to successfully compete against someone who loves what they do. This is because while you may very well consider the work that you do necessary to gain a competitive advantage, your rival considers the work pleasurable and, in many instances, doesn't consider it to be work at all. As a result, while you necessarily will need to take regular, frequent breaks from your work to concentrate on enjoyable activities, your rival will require much less "down time" because she is already doing what she loves. Eventually, you cannot compete with such a person.

Of course, even people who love what they do are not immune from stress and fatigue. However, they are more likely to bounce back quickly because, underneath it all, the nature of the work is inherently satisfying to them. Since the unhappy lawyer does not have a similarly firm foundation from which to find support (after all, *his* stress and fatigue is only further compounded by the fact that he takes no innate pleasure in the substance of his work), eventual failure is a foregone conclusion.

Perhaps you've picked up this book with the hope that you'd discover a few "tricks" to ensuring success as a practicing lawyer. If so, here is the best trick of all: despite the competitive scenario described above, the surest way to achieve partnership or the promotion you desire has nothing to do with defeating that happy, satisfied fellow associate. Rather, the trick *is to become that person.* For while you cannot win while competing against one of them, you likewise cannot lose if you are that person. Because to you, it won't feel as if you are competing at all. Rather, you'll spend your days doing what you love and accepting the stresses and headaches that invariably crop up as minor unpleasantries that, although need to be dealt with, will eventually pass. In the end, you cannot help but advance because, as the above example illustrates, it was an unfair competition to begin with. The other guy just never had a chance.

Professional Happiness is More Than Just a Mushy Concept

By now you've probably heard a professor or two during college or law school wax philosophically about the evils of working merely to make money. Perhaps you agreed wholeheartedly. Or, more likely, perhaps you agreed in principle but concluded that in reality, such lofty notions are best kept within the safe confines of the ivory tower. Because as everyone knows, money makes so many other things in life possible. So while it would be great to enjoy what you do, perhaps you ultimately concluded that a nice paycheck would allow you to achieve happiness in other ways; ways unrelated to how you earn a living. Unfortunately, if you've chosen the practice of law as your profession, this is simply an impossibility.

First of all, given the sheer number of hours attorneys work, there is not enough quality time left in the day to spend your money on other enjoyable activities on a regular basis. While having the ability to afford a European vacation every year is certainly nice, it is important to remember that that trip will occupy, at most, two weeks out of the year. Now ask yourself: does it make sense to force yourself to endure 50 miserable weeks just so that you'll be able to enjoy the other two? Moreover, while an expensive car is fun, is it worth spending 12 torturous hours each day working for it just so you can enjoy the 20 minute ride to and from work? There isn't enough free time during the day or enough vacation time during the year to justify a miserable existence at work. The math just doesn't add up.

More importantly, however, is that working merely to make money will only lead to frustration, not merely regarding professional satisfaction issues but eventually, frustration over money itself.

17

One of the most universal truisms in the work world is that no matter how much money you make, there will always be somebody who makes more (unless, of course, you're Bill Gates). If you are otherwise satisfied with your job, this financial disparity might be an occasional annoyance but nothing more. Because underneath it all, you love what you do. If, however, your professional goal is to simply make as much money as possible, you can't help but be frustrated when comparing yourself with those who make more. Because, after all, there is no other reason for you to get out of bed in the morning. Even if you assume for a moment that everything previously discussed in this chapter is false and that it is possible to succeed if you do not love what you do, by definition you have *still* failed professionally because, since there are people in your field earning more than you, *you are not making as much money as possible.* By defining success solely in financial terms, you have made achievement of success an impossibility. And nothing in the world can be more frustrating than that. Of course, given that everything previously discussed is indeed true, the individual working solely for a paycheck will find that his frustration level rises even exponentially higher because he most likely will be stuck in a lower or mid-level position due to his failure to successfully compete with those who enjoy what they do.

Finally, for those who still need further evidence that professional happiness is a prerequisite to success and more than just a corny ideal, a chat with a leader in his or her field of interest is probably a good idea. After taking the time to listen to these people, it will become clear that a love of the work itself, rather than a desire for riches, is what motivates them. This is particularly true in the practice of law where the work is just too demanding to be done merely for the paycheck. Simply stated, there are dozens of easier ways to earn a comfortable living. Contrary to the popular perception, the average lawyer earns less than the average corporate middle manager and works many more hours and countless weekends. Those who rise to the top of the legal profession typically work even longer hours than most lawyers but do so not because they want to earn the most but because they find what they do enjoyable.

Many law firms are dotted with partners who could have retired years earlier but choose to continue practicing out of sheer love of the work. A young associate in a large Philadelphia firm tells the story of a senior partner well into his 70's who still roams his firm's halls, barking out advice to the younger associates while carrying a full caseload. More often than not, the senior partner is already behind his desk by the time the associate arrives in the morning and is still hard at work late into the evening when the associate leaves for home. When asked why he continued to work so hard when he could so easily retire on his comfortable pension, this senior partner replied that to him, there was nothing he'd rather do than try cases. Another firm employed a partner who came to work every day well into his 90's. To him, the practice of law brought emotional fulfillment rather than merely a paycheck every two weeks. Firms in every community are filled with similar examples. In fact, one of the most pressing issues facing law firms today is how to respond to the growing multitude of older attorneys who have past the age of retirement but still choose to practice. Although at first glance it may appear to be an unsolvable contradiction that the same profession known so famously for professional dissatisfaction can be the same one which has great trouble encouraging its older members to leave, in reality there is no contradiction at all. Rather, because the practice of law is a competitive one, young attorneys are naturally subjected to a weeding-out process where the unhappy ones are eventually eliminated and the happy ones remain and prosper. Consequently, staying power (and ultimately success, financial and otherwise) is the direct result of professional happiness rather than the cause. Regardless of your personal beliefs regarding the innate value of professional happiness, hopefully this chapter has shown that, at least with respect to the practice of law, to ignore the emotional satisfaction factor is to do so at your peril.

Chapter Two: Beware the Pigeonhole

Although you may have never thought of it this way, your initial legal job after graduation from law school marks the commencement of not your first, but rather, your *second* career. From the time you entered kindergarten through your final law school exam, you were hard at work in your first career: that of a student. By the time you've graduated from law school, you've spent a minimum of 20 years working as a student and learning the in's and out's of that trade. Perhaps the most important lesson learned during this time was the one preached to you by parents and teachers alike and the one you no doubt saw in action; i.e, that more education brings more opportunities while less education limits professional choices down the road. Therefore, as a career student with two decades of practice, it most likely has become ingrained in you that experience, and the educational opportunities that naturally flow from it, can only be beneficial and can only serve to widen your professional choices in the future. In the practice of law, however, it is often the case that just the opposite is true. In the legal job market, experience is a typically a limiting, rather than a broadening, factor. As a result, many unsuspecting young lawyers who most likely accepted positions in firms on the assumption that the experience could only help them down the road find themselves pigeonholed in areas of law they find uninteresting with no way of getting out.

As a career student, you are most likely comfortable with the concept of jumping blindly into new experiences because, up to now, new experiences have always represented educational opportunities with little or no accompanying risk. For example, while you may not have known exactly what you were getting into when applying to and choosing a college, you knew that in the end, you would have more professional choices as a college graduate than a high school graduate. Similarly, when applying to law school, you may not have known what the "practice of law" specifically entailed, but you were probably aware that those with law degrees earn significantly more and find jobs much more easily than those with merely bachelor degrees.

Likewise, you may feel that the same rules apply when searching for that first job after law school. Therefore, while you may not know exactly what "insurance coverage litigation" is, you probably would not fret too much over this if your law firm of choice offered you a position in that department. You, like many other law students, would most likely accept the position, figuring that if the past is any guide, the job would be, at worst, an educational experience which could only broaden the range of potential job choices down the road. This time, however, your "blind jump" would be a disastrous mistake.

Although, given everything you know up to now, it only makes sense that those with a few years of experience would be more attractive to potential employers than those right out of law school, it is important to understand that in the "business" of law, the rules are dramatically different from anything you've seen before. As the following section will show, a young lawyer who accepts a position in a particular department of a firm is not opening himself up to yet another educationally broadening experience, but, rather, from the perspective of the legal job market, has made a decision which limits his future career choices to that field (and perhaps a limited number of very closely related ones). Consequently, if a few years down the road the young lawyer discovers that he does not like his chosen field, he will have an extremely difficult time switching to another one. Because the legal job market is counter-intuitive from everything you've learned up to now, it is very easy to find yourself pigeonholed despite your best efforts to broaden your experience. In short, for the first time in your life, jumping blindly can be professionally deadly.

How Pigeonholing Works

In order to understand just how it is that young attorneys can get themselves locked into a particular practice area without their knowledge, it is important to understand how the legal job market changes from the time you take your first job right out of law school to the time you re-enter the market a few years later, this time with professional experience.

A. The Job Market for Newly-Graduated Attorneys

Since many first jobs are acquired as a result of a law student's successful internship during the summer after his or her second year of law school (albeit fewer now than prior to the most recent economic downturn), an analysis of the summer internship process as a whole is necessary to understand the range of professional choices available to law students.

During this summer, some law students take a position in medium to large law firms where they are expected to learn about "firm life" and make decisions regarding their particular field of interest. Accordingly, some firms (although fewer now than in previous decades) set up a formal "rotation" program whereby summer associates spend a few weeks in each department in order to get a better understanding of the type of work handled by each department within the firm. Other firms have a less rigid structure and create, instead, a summer associate assignment "pool" wherein assignments from every department collect. It is up to the summer associate to select the assignments which pique his or her interest although summer associates are usually advised to select a wide range of assignments in order to get a realistic feel for the type of work done in the various departments.

Assuming that the summer goes well (and, statistically speaking, summers usually go well for summer associates, given that most firms offer permanent positions to the overwhelming majority of their summer associate class), the summer typically ends with an exit interview wherein the summer associate is expected to choose the department in which she would prefer to work. While the choice of departments is, of course, dependant upon positions available within each department, most larger firms expect each of their departments to take in at least one entry-level associate every year. Therefore, for the summer associate coming off a successful internship, a position in the firm's product liability group is just as attainable as a position within the taxation department as is a position within the entertainment law group, and so on. Although a firm may prefer a particular summer associate join a particular group and attempt to convince them to do so, ultimately the decision is typically up to the summer associate. The range of possibilities is limited only by the range of departments within a given firm. Whatever area of law floats the summer associate's boat is usually fine with the firm. All of this changes, however, a few years down the road.

And what of those folks whose first and/or summer jobs are with smaller firms or sole practitioners? Although the accoutrements of these firms might be less glamorous and the range of practice options within each particular firm more limited (and, unfortunately, the salary more modest), candidates seeking summer or permanent employment here are still likely to find themselves with a wide range of options available to them. Although one small firm might handle only domestic matters and another only criminal cases, taken as a whole, the small firm/sole practitioner employment market offers a vast array of career choices to the law student or freshly graduated candidate. And here, just as in the larger firms, prospective employers are simply looking for a hard-working, capable person who demonstrates potential. Even if a particular candidate has just graduated from law school with a concentration in corporate law, his ability to land a first job at a small family law firm won't be adversely affected so long as his would-be employer sees him as a congenial, industrious worker with a willingness to learn. As a newly-minted-grad, whether you're seeking employment with a mega-firm or a sole practitioner, your range of career options is limited only by your imagination. You can decide that you want to be a corporate lawyer one week, a criminal lawyer the next, and an entertainment lawyer the week after that if you so choose. All that is required of you is the motivation to seek out those firms that offer what you want. For the most part, firms of any size don't care about your specific experience all that much at this stage of your legal career; to them it's potential that matters most – that spark that shows them that you have the ability to grow into your job, regardless of the specificities of your law school career (other than grades, that is).

B. The Job Market For Experienced Attorneys

Once this young attorney accepts his position, however, the dynamics shift enormously, although imperceptibly until it is too late. And once this now experienced attorney hits the legal job market again, most likely after only two to three years at his initial firm, he will find that the range of choices available to him are limited to his current area of practice – a frustrating prospect given that it was his dislike of his current area of practice which caused him to seek other employment in the first place. Unfortunately, there is not much he can do about it at this point.

From the perspective of the young attorney, this does not seem to make sense. After all, only a few short years ago, he had his choice of legal fields. He could have just as easily chosen one field as another. And this was when he was inexperienced. Now, given all he has learned with a few years of (for example) corporate litigation experience under his belt, he is eminently better qualified to handle the work in any other area of the law. However, the hiring attorneys in these areas are no longer view him as a viable candidate. How he could be qualified for a position in, let's say, medical malpractice litigation with no experience but unqualified for the same position with three years of experience seems beyond reason. It is not until this young attorney's candidacy is understood from the perspective of these seemingly nitwitted hiring partners does it become clear just why it is that this young attorney is such an unattractive candidate.

1. The Hiring Partner's Perspective

When it comes to choosing among job candidates, a hiring partner's job is to get the most "bang" for her firm's buck. That is, it is her job to see to it that her firm's resources (financial as well as training) are utilized in the most efficient, economic way. Among entry-level hires, her job is a relatively easy one since every student comes to the firm with roughly the same skills. It is assumed that students are essentially clueless when it comes to knowledge of substantive law in their practice area of choice regardless of the number of courses a particular student has taken in a specific legal niche during law school. Therefore, it makes little practical difference to the hiring partner whether a particular student wants to join the litigation or trusts and estates department; the firm will most likely spend similar training resources regardless. (Small firms and sole practitioners are no different in this regard – the hiring attorney must assume that he or she will have to spend significant time and money training newly-minted grads to become "practice-ready" regardless of the content of their law school transcripts. This explains why many of these firms are hesitant to hire such candidates in the first place and often prefer more experienced attorneys – those who have already been pigeonholed, for better or worse). Likewise, salary concerns are non-existent when it comes to the law student hiring process since most firms start every first year associate at the same salary, regardless of department. In short, when it comes to hiring law students, the law student's practice area of preference makes little difference to the hiring partner since the costs are relatively fixed. As long as there is an opening in a particular department and so long as the student made an overall favorable impression on the firm during his summer clerkship or interview, he is generally free to select the department of his choice.

A few years down the road, however, everything changes. Now, when (for example) a third year associate hits the market, the training and financial costs are no longer fixed. As a result, it will be the candidate who costs the firm the least in terms of training resources plus salary who will always get the job. By definition, it will never be the person seeking to switch areas of law.

2. The Law Firm's Decision-making Process

For example, let's examine a mythical opening in the medical malpractice department of a large firm. There are three candidates for the position: a third year associate presently practicing medical malpractice litigation at another firm, the corporate litigator discussed earlier, likewise with three years of experience, and a newly-minted law school graduate who has just passed the bar. Each of the candidates comes highly recommended. Who should the hiring partner select?

Between the two associates with equivalent experience, it is an easy decision. Given that one associate has relevant medical malpractice litigation experience, she will be the one who will cost the firm less in terms of training. She will be the one who will provide the most bang for the firm's buck. While some young attorneys who want to switch fields believe that they will be able to override this equation by promising to work for less money, this is rarely a viable option for a firm. Law firms (particularly medium and larger firms), like most corporations, have rigid, regimented salary structures that are, for the most part, inflexible. A third year associate must earn a third year salary in order to maintain the integrity of the firm's salary structure. While there are ranges for each salary grade which take into account individual performance and other factors, it is rarely the case that a firm will be able to pay an attorney with three years experience a first year's salary. There are some small firms that may be able to accommodate such a salary/experience discrepancy but for the most part, this practice is frowned upon.

As a result, the attorney with corporate litigation experience is not preferred by the hiring partner because hiring him would result in the firm expending training resources (which include time as well as money) to bring him up to the competence level of the associate who already has medical malpractice experience. Since the firm is otherwise committed to paying a third year salary to either candidate, this additional strain on training resources makes the corporate litigation associate an unattractive candidate.

Let's take the experienced medical malpractice candidate out of the picture for a moment and assume that there are only two candidates for the medical malpractice position – the third year corporate litigator and the newly-minted grad. Here as well it is an easy decision for the firm but, to the shock and dismay of the more experienced associate, he comes out on the short end once again. Why? This time, although training resources would be roughly equivalent, the more experienced associate would cost more in terms of salary than the newly-minted grad. It just doesn't make sense from a hiring partner's perspective to pay someone a third year's salary if the firm will then have to train that person as if he were a first year associate. Although the third year associate would probably require slightly less training than the newly-minted grad, it ordinarily would not be enough of a difference to offset the difference in salaries.

Changing this hypothetical by increasing the level of experience (and, consequently, reducing the amount of training required) of the seasoned associate doesn't change the analysis. If one were to assume that a sixth year associate would require substantially less training in a new field of law than a third year associate, she would still be a less attractive option than the newly-minted grad because while the training cost differential now tilts somewhat more in the sixth year associate's favor, the salary differential weighs significantly on the newly-minted grad's. The difference between a first year salary and a sixth year's, at small firms as well as large ones, can be enormous. Thus, the more experienced associate can never close the gap between her marketability and that of the newly-minted grad's. The less training she requires, the more salary she commands, whether she wants it or not. By the time she has enough experience to switch from one area of law to another with practically no training, the salary difference between herself and a newly-minted grad's would be so great as to make even considering her for the position to be cost-prohibitive from the firm's perspective. The experienced attorney can never win this competition.

Now let's bring the third year associate with medical malpractice litigation experience back into the discussion. Between her and the newly-minted grad, the decision becomes more difficult and complex. Depending on what the firm is looking for (someone to step right in and handle complex litigation versus someone who can be groomed for the future), the hiring partner might decide to save on training and take on the higher salary or, conversely, invest the firm's resources in training and save in salary. In this competition, who gets the job will likely depend both on the firm's needs at the moment as well as the firm's overall impressions of the two candidates.

Under any scenario, the attorney who ultimately gets a particular job will be the one who either has direct, relevant experience or who expresses an interest in that particular field without bringing the baggage that comes with experience in another area of law. As a current law student, it is your job to identify your legal field of interest now, before you acquire the baggage that will only hinder you down the road. Failure today to consider the attractiveness of your candidacy a few years down the road may very well result in your being pigeonholed for the rest of your career. How to identify your field of interest will be discussed in depth in *Chapter 4: How to Make Sure That You Do What You Love.*

Escaping Your Pigeonhole

One thing you should take from this book is that it is never too late. No matter how dire your professional situation, there is always a way out of it. The theme of this book is not simply that your fate is determined in law school so thus, anyone reading this book after graduation is doomed to a lifetime of misery. Instead, the theme is that choices are made more easily in law school than afterwards and, given the forces conspiring against change in the legal world, it is easier to plan for happiness while still in school than as a professional. However, this does not mean that meaningful career changes cannot take place even several years after graduation. These changes will just take much longer to implement; years rather than the mere moments they would have taken back when you were a student. But they can be made and, more importantly, they *should* be made. This section will discuss what to do if you're in the workforce and need to climb out of your pigeonhole. It should also serve as a warning to those still in school who will see just how much more difficult and time-consuming it becomes to change the focus of your career once you leave law school.

One thing you most certainly *should not* do if you find yourself pigeonholed and want to get out is to jump right in to the job market hoping that lightning will strike and that you somehow will defy the odds and land your dream job in your preferred field of interest. This chapter has shown that your likelihood of success is extremely remote. You are at a competitive disadvantage against the vast majority of other folks who likewise have applied for the position. Many people believe that simply tossing their hat into the ring is worthwhile because at least they're doing *something* and not merely sitting back, complaining about their current job. In fact, given that they stand almost no chance of landing that job, it is as if they were doing nothing. Printing out a resume and putting a stamp on an envelope is not nearly the extent of the effort required to bring about meaningful changes in your professional life.

Instead, climbing out of your pigeonhole requires you to create a new pigeonhole for yourself, one that *you* create rather than the one that was created previously for you. This requires you to essentially work two jobs for a period of time: the one in which you are currently unhappy and a new one which involves the type of work you hope to transition into one day. Oftentimes, you will not be paid for this "extra job." Sometimes, this "extra job" will even cost you money. However, in the long run, you will gain enough relevant experience in your preferred field of interest to make yourself attractive to hiring partners. You will be able to convince them that hiring you will not cause them to expend significant training resources and you will likewise justify your salary. You will become competitive with your rivals in both training and salary costs and, as such, will present yourself as the candidate who gives the hiring partner the aforementioned most "bang for the buck." It may take a few years to get to this point, but in the end, all of that hard work will be worth it. How to create your new pigeonhole? Here are two ways:

A. Take on Pro Bono Cases in Your Field of Interest

Alice B. is a good example of how to effectively escape an unwanted pigeonhole by creating a more favorable one and then utilizing the new pigeonhole to land that dream job. Alice was an associate in a large insurance defense firm. She spent four years as an associate at this firm, handling medical malpractice and other, smaller personal injury cases. From the time she was in law school, however, she had an interest in family law. This interest increased as she grew frustrated with the type of work she was now doing and in which she never had an interest.

Although her firm did not have a family law department (and, even if it did, it is the rare occasion when a firm permits an associate to switch departments in the absence of extraordinary circumstances-i.e., circumstances which benefit the firm rather than the associate) she found a non-profit children's rights organization which would allow her to take cases pro bono. At first she took one case, then a few, then a few more. Although these cases did not count toward her firm's billable hour requirement, they helped her gain experience and credibility within the family law community in her city. Eventually, after a few years, she was able to use the connections she made while working pro bono to get herself an interview with a family law firm and eventually a job. At some point along the way, people began to see her as a family lawyer rather than as a personal injury lawyer. Once that shift in mindset was complete, it was relatively easy for her to land her dream job. Simply mailing a resume to a family law firm (or even a hundred family law firms) would never have gotten her to her preferred destination.

B. Consider Returning to School to Establish Credibility in Your Field of Interest

Charles D. took a somewhat different path to breaking out of his pigeonhole and creating a new one, but an equally effective one. Charles was a mid-level insurance coverage associate in a large firm who wished to be a corporate lawyer instead. Although he knew what he wanted to do back when he was in law school, he took a position in the insurance coverage litigation department because he believed that he would be able to eventually transition into his firm's corporate department (please see Chapter Four to learn how to avoid being sweet-talked into a job that promises more than it can deliver). By the time he realized that this was not going to happen, he had already become pigeonholed as an insurance coverage attorney. Although pro bono corporate cases exist (most major cities have groups that help low income people operate businesses, assist with their legal problems, etc.), they're typically not as readily available as the family law cases of which Alice was able to avail herself. So instead, Charles decided to go back to school to get his MBA.

Many people believe (and these people are generally correct) that a law degree trumps an MBA so therefore, it makes little sense for someone who already is an attorney to return to school to get what is perceived to be a lesser degree. However, Charles needed his MBA not merely to acquire business skills but to show the legal community that he was a *business lawyer* rather than an insurance coverage attorney. Receiving that degree would help do the trick.

Returning to school at this point in his professional career was not an easy decision. He was married with young children and would not have the luxury of leaving his unpleasant job to return to school full time. As a result, it would take four years (with all of his classes taking place during the evenings and weekends) for him to get his degree rather than the standard two. Moreover, it was expensive. However, he believed that this investment in time and money was necessary for him to break out of his mold and forge a new identity.

Although he gave up most of his evenings and weekends for the next four years, and added several thousands of dollars to his student loans, he was in fact able to change the legal community's perception of him. After graduation, he was able to transition from the insurance coverage position he previously held to the corporate counsel position he dreamed of back when he was a law student. It may have taken many years and many thousands of dollars, but he eventually got to where he wanted to be.

Alice and Charles show that it is never too late. Meaningful career change can take place at any time, if you want to change badly enough. Alice and Charles also show, however, that meaningful change can take years to effect once you've begun your professional career. Back when they were in law school, Alice could have just as easily taken a position at a family law firm as the personal injury litigation position she eventually accepted. Charles could have refused his firm's offer to join its' insurance coverage litigation department and held out for a corporate law position. The consequences of their failure to accept the positions offered them would have been relatively minor: they would not have the security of having a job in their pocket as early as they did, so they would have had to keep looking, perhaps for a few more weeks or months.

A few short years later, however, the consequences of their having accepted these positions were enormous. Each person invested years and significant amounts of money (either explicitly, as Charles did, or implicitly as Alice did by spending time on pro bono cases rather than on fee-generating cases which would have resulted in bigger raises at the end of each year) working to undo the damage caused by their mistake. Although they did not realize it at the time, the experience they gained by working in areas of the law that were emotionally unsatisfying to them did nothing to help them but everything to hurt them both now and quite possibly for the rest of their professional lives. It was only through their perseverance and dedication to changing their careers that they were able to climb out of their pigeonholes and create new identities for themselves. If only they were aware of these pigeonholes back when they were students, the next several years of their lives would have been much happier.

Chapter Three: Working With Your Career Services Office

Many unhappy lawyers lay the blame for their woes solely at the feet of their law school's career services office. "They should have warned me," they believe. "They obviously knew that my firm was a sweatshop and that real estate law was boring. And that I would be stuck doing this forever with no hope of ever changing practice areas. Why didn't they tell me?" Since their career is not going well, it is only logical to assume that the career *services* office must be to blame. For clearly, it failed to service their career adequately. What these unhappy lawyers fail to realize is that they did not give their career services office an adequate opportunity to help them. If provided with the appropriate information, and if presented with clear, specific career goals by a student, your career services office very often can do extraordinary things to help students who know what they want get where they want to go. If, however, provided with nothing more than a student who wants a job, any job, it more often than not will place that student in an ill-fitting position that will quickly develop into a pigeonhole (see Chapter Two) out of which there is little hope for escape. It is up to you, not your career services office, to make sure that this does not happen.

Your Career Services Office *Does* Want to Help You

For starters, understand that your career services office wants you to succeed and be happy. In fact, many career guidance counselors see their primary role (if not their *only* role) as helping students identify and reach their career goals. It's just that, when given very little to work with, they are unable to produce much in the way of satisfactory results in this regard.

The process of purchasing a car provides a helpful analogy. If you, the buyer, walked into a dealership and told the salesperson nothing more than that you wanted to buy a car, she would do what she could to help you achieve this goal. She would probably direct you to whatever model she had overstocked and send you off on a test ride. In the end, she'd sell you a car, but probably the one she wanted to get rid of rather than the one you really wanted. If, however, you told the salesperson what you were looking for in a car, what you expected it to do for you, she would direct you to something which approximated your expectations. The more information you were able to provide to the salesperson, the better able she'd be to provide you with exactly what you were looking for. In the end, you'd stand a greater chance of driving off with the car of your dreams. In either scenario, the salesperson would be equally happy for having made a sale. Your happiness, on the other hand, would vary greatly.

Too many students walk into their career offices asking for nothing more than a car. Regardless of the state of the economy, the job market for new attorneys is almost always described by anxious law students as a bad one; one in which beggars cannot afford to be choosers. As a result, the talk in the law school's corridors revolves around merely finding a generic "job." To hold out for something better than what's being offered is considered bad form and foolhardy. A job, any job, is the goal of most students. Given these expectations, it is no wonder that most students get nothing more than what they asked for.

The truth is that the state of the "job market" is largely irrelevant to your ability to land a job in a legal area which matches your interests. While "bad jobs" (the jobs nobody wants anyway) might be somewhat harder to get in a down market, the good ones are always going to prove somewhat elusive, regardless of the state of the economy. Those who don't shoot for them will never get them (they'll never fall into their laps by accident), but those who do stand a good chance of landing them no matter how bad the economy. The trick is to use your career services office to help you undertake a focused search which ferrets out the job of your dreams.

Differentiating Between the Bad Jobs and the Good Ones

Before you can enlist the aid of your career services office, you'll need to be able to tell the difference between a good job and a bad one. Contrary to popular perception, a good job is not merely one which has been offered to you. As you learned in Chapter Two, accepting the wrong job out of law school can have enormous, long term negative consequences. Instead, you need to evaluate what's out there and weed out those jobs that are nothing more than a paycheck (and, as discussed in Chapter One, a frustrating paycheck at that).

So what constitutes a bad job? For starters, you would do well to assume that those jobs most readily available are probably not the most desirous. After all, they're available for a reason. Although most medium to large law firms yearly anticipate hiring a new associate to each of their departments, they need more young associates in those departments requiring a greater amount of grunt work (sorting through voluminous boxes of documents, assisting as the junior associate on huge cases staffed by multiple attorneys, etc.). If the "grunt work" is in an area of law which you have an interest, great. That job may very well be a good fit for you. Everyone has to start somewhere and "pay their dues" and you will be no different.

If, however, the "grunt work" is in an area of law that does not interest you, the job is a bad one and you should stay away from it, regardless of the salary. As stated in Chapter One, law firms consciously hire many more associates than they could ever hope to promote to partnership. Many of these "extra" associates are junior associates in these departments who are hired to do the work more seasoned attorneys prefer not to do (and who, realistically, cannot do in the eyes of the client, given their higher hourly rates). Law firms hire these associates understanding that many of them will leave within a few years, having burned out on the sheer drudgery of the work. While these hires are nevertheless profitable for the law firm, they are disastrous to the young attorneys who leave, given that their career options are then extremely limited.

Due to the burnout factor, these jobs are almost always plentiful (the exception being a particularly distressed economy when, because current associates and paralegals are compelled to assume a larger share of this grunt work in the firm's effort to save money, they are the first to be eliminated). They also pay well -- in many cases, the highest paying jobs will come from here. Except for the select few who find the substantive areas of law behind the grunt work interesting, they are also bad jobs. Returning to an earlier analogy, these jobs are the cars offered to you if you ask for nothing more than employment. To the extent that your career services office is overstocked with any type of job, it is with this type. These are the jobs many employers are selling when they come on campus to interview. These are the easiest ones for your career services office to place: the employers are already on campus, looking to make offers (except, as stated above, when, due to the economy, these jobs dry up. This results in the reduced number of campus law firm interviews that receive so much attention). Your career services office rarely has to do more than facilitate the interview process in order to fill them. It seems almost too easy to get a good job this way. As is the case everywhere else, when something seems too good to be true, it usually is. Just as when you're buying a car, remember the time-honored motto: caveat emptor – buyer beware.

The good jobs, by contrast, will usually be the ones that are not broadcast so loudly. They most likely will not be the ones brought to you on a silver platter during the on-campus recruiting season. This doesn't mean that the firms coming to your school will never offer positions in your field of choice, it just means that you'll need to do a little work to identify and ferret them out. Discussing and negotiating the position of your choice with a law firm will be addressed in Chapter Four. Before you get to that point, however, you need to do some homework. And here is where your career services office can be your greatest ally in your quest for future happiness. Here is where you give your career services counselor the opportunity to sell you the car of your dreams rather than whatever she's got sitting around on the lot.

How to Work With Your Career Services Office

By now you know that you cannot simply walk into your career services office, fall to your knees in supplication, and hope that the counselors will magically find you the job of your dreams. To begin with, this is your job, not theirs. Furthermore, even if it was their job, it would be impossible for them to succeed given that you have not provided any helpful information to assist them. Therefore, you need to do your homework before walking in so that you'll be able to help them help you.

You'll need to go above and beyond the typical law student in utilizing the career services office. The first way you'll do this is by actually sitting down and speaking with one of the counselors. Too many students skip this important step, focusing instead solely on the on-campus interview program and other job-hunting postings. These features are useless if you do not already know what area of law you're interested in. All they will do is land you a job in which you'll be unhappily pigeonholed within a couple of years. Many students mistakenly believe that the counseling aspect of their career services office is only for those students who are either completely clueless as to what they want to do with their lives or those students interested in clerkships or public interest positions. To the contrary, your career services office is there to help *you*, regardless of your professional aspirations.

If you have no idea what area of law interests you professionally, of course the career services office is a great place to *start* your research. Your counselor can administer tests that match your personality with the tasks involved in various types of jobs. She can initiate a dialogue that will help you focus more sharply on your career objectives. These tools will provide you with a sound jumping-off point for the more specific research you'll then need to do.

Once you have some idea of your interests (see Chapter Four for help in identifying your interests), you can use the career services office to help confirm your interest or disavow you of some of your assumptions. Come to the meeting with your counselor prepared with specific questions regarding your area of interest. Then fire away. Don't be embarrassed to ask anything. Too many students are afraid to admit that they have absolutely no idea what the practice of law is like. Instead, they hold their assumptions (formed most likely through the sensationalized attorneys they've seen on television and in movies) inside and present a façade of complete and total understanding of what they're getting themselves into.

In reality, since you are still a student, you cannot reasonably be expected to know what life is like after graduation. While your career services counselor may not be able to answer every specific question you may have, she will probably be able to utilize your school's vast alumni network to put you in touch with someone who can. The fact that this person may very well become an important contact who will enable you to eventually land the job of your dreams is an additional bonus. For this reason, be certain to ask for this type of information and make sure to leave your meeting with the names of at least a few such alumni. They can only help you down the road.

When you have a clearer picture of the area of law in which you are interested, go back to the career services office again, this time with a list of the specific firms that practice in this area. Ask your counselor about each one. What is the reputation of each firm? What is it known for? Is the counselor aware of anyone who has had a negative experience with the firm? What happened? Why? Again, she may not be able to answer all of your questions but she probably will be able to direct you to alumni who either work there or who may be familiar with it. Just as before, these people will be valuable to you not only in the information they provide to your specific questions but as resources down the road when you finally are ready to shoot for a particular position at a particular firm.

Use Your Career Services Office to Gain Access to Influential Alumni

As you are no doubt noticing, your career services office is not merely a clearinghouse for jobs, it is your link to the vast network of influential alumni who may be able to help you land the right job for you. These alumni may not be the hiring partners in their firms, but given that they have made themselves accessible to your career services office, they obviously have an interest in helping to place graduates from their alma mater in their firms. They may be aware of potential job openings in your area of interest that are not heavily advertised. They may be able to "pull a few strings" to help make a position available in the Antitrust Group, for example, where previously none existed. They are invaluable. They are also for the most part unreachable to you without the aid of your career services office.

Most likely, your career services counselor will give you the telephone number of an alumnus and ask you to proceed directly on your own. If so, try to use the telephone call to set up a face-to-face meeting. Try to avoid making the phone call the extent of your interaction. Although it is easier to speak to someone you do not know over the phone than in-person, and

44

while you may be able to get all of your specific questions answered over the phone, you will not be able to establish the sort of relationship wherein your alumni contact will be willing to use her influence to help you land the job of your dreams. It is rare that a stranger will be able to make the sort of impression on someone through a telephone call (or worse, an exchange of emails) that will motivate that person to take the extra step to help them get a job. This type of influence can only result through an extended, personal, interaction. Use the phone call to ask your contact to lunch. Offer to pay (don't worry, your contact will probably insist on paying at the end of the meal anyway. And if she does not, you've spent a relatively few dollars to gain the influence of someone who may change your life). Be extremely flexible as to available dates and times. Whenever and wherever she can meet is fine with you. The point is to make personal contact and hold her attention for at least an hour.

When you finally sit down with your alumni contact, don't be afraid to ask the tough questions. While you want to make a positive impression on her, avoid the temptation to treat the meeting as a de facto interview. Rest assured that your alumni contact does not consider your meeting to be an interview. If an interview was all you wanted, she'd no doubt refer you to the firm's hiring partner, politely ask you to send in a resume and then end the conversation. Instead, treat the meeting as purely informational. After all, you are there first and foremost to find out more about a particular area of law or a particular firm. You cannot find this type of information out by asking "softball" questions. If she reacts defensively, then you've probably discovered the answer to your questions right there. If, however, she gives you a reasoned, well-thought-out response, it may change what might have been an unfair negative perception on your part. And, given that asking and answering tough questions is what the practice of law is all about, she will probably be impressed by the thoughtfulness and depth of your inquiries. This can only help you later on.

Try to set up as many of these alumni meetings as possible. Don't be afraid to return to your career services office repeatedly to ask for additional alumni contacts. Use these meetings to teach yourself as much as you can about the areas of law in which you may be interested. Write down what you learned after each meeting as well as all necessary contact information. You may need that later when you explicitly and officially start your job search and you'd be surprised how quick and easy it is to lose such information. Use what you learned at prior meetings in subsequent ones. This will enable you to ask precise questions that will give you the detailed information you'll need to make an informed career decision.

Finally, regardless of how well or poorly any particular meeting goes, remember to be courteous at all times. Even if you feel that your alumni contact wasn't as forthcoming as she should have been, or if she was just plain rude or non-communicative, thank her for her time. Even in the largest cities, the legal profession is an amazingly close one. Everybody seems to know everybody else. You cannot afford to risk your future by being impolite. You have no idea who your contact knows, who she has influence with. Remember that while an influential alumnus can pull some strings to help you get a job, she can also exert extraordinary influence to prevent you from getting one as well if she sets her mind to it. Never give such a person a reason to do so. As this book shows, landing the job of your dreams requires work on your part. Having somebody influential working against you only doubles or triples the amount of work required. It is simply not worth it.

The same can be said with regard to your career services office. When used properly, it can open doors to you that would otherwise remain closed. It can be the gateway to a lifetime of professional happiness. If, however, you make use of its services without fully understanding how to properly go about it, you can very quickly find yourself in a negative employment situation with little hope of escaping. By understanding what your career services office requires of you in order for it to be of effective assistance, you can better utilize it to achieve your goals. You will be well on your way to becoming the happy lawyer you always wanted to become.

Chapter Four: How to Make Sure That You Do What You Love

Everybody talks about doing what they love while they are in law school, yet most people end up doing something else entirely. There are several reasons as to why this happens, many of which have already been discussed in this book. Some people believe that happiness is a noble yet unattainable goal at the embryonic stage of their career and that happiness will naturally evolve as they gain experience and stature. This allows them to accept less in a job than would otherwise be the case and remain there despite their dissatisfaction. Some people believe that while they may not enjoy what they do today, their choices will expand as their skills develop. Still others believe that it is their definition of happiness which is the problem and that their perception of professional happiness as a student was idealistic and naïve. These people eventually condition themselves to accept their professional roles and settle for something far less than they had hoped for as students, conveniently matching their current jobs with their revised, downsized notion of professional satisfaction. While there may be many reasons why a particular person chooses to do something other than what they love, all of these people have one thing in common: they are all, to some degree, dissatisfied.

There is nothing inherently different about the practice of law that causes so many of its practitioners to bemoan their lot in life. Moreover, unlike virtually any other field, the law touches virtually every aspect of society, every other profession, all of the arts and any avocation under the sun. To dislike "the law" is to find nothing stimulating in any other aspect of waking life as well. Regardless, many lawyers will not hesitate to denigrate their profession, laying the blame for their professional unhappiness entirely on "the law" as an abstract concept rather than on the strong likelihood that they have simply made a fundamental mistake in the determination of their specific area of practice. Of course, as discussed in Chapter Two, since many lawyers had their specific area of practice selected for them and have never had the opportunity to examine the vast array of professional choices available to someone with a law degree, it is not surprising that they fail to see their choice of fields (or lack thereof) as the predominant factor in their unhappiness.

It is as easy to find a legal field you find stimulating and enjoyable as it is to identify what you find stimulating and enjoyable in life itself. The two are intertwined in a way which can only benefit you if you take advantage of the opportunities available to you as a law school graduate and are not afraid to shoot for what you love rather than settle for something less. It is only the person who believes that personal and professional interests are separate universes who is doomed to a life of emotional compromises and unrealized dreams. Unfortunately, because of the damage caused by pigeonholing in the legal profession, a great number of lawyers fall into this category, lawyers who once thought differently but who are now resigned to the idea that professional happiness in the law is merely a mirage. Chapters One through

Three have shown why this is not and, more importantly, *cannot*, be the case. Now you will learn how to ensure that it will not be the case in your life either.

<u>Identify What You Enjoy and Then Go Do It</u>

A. The Value of Professional Personality Profiling Techniques

There are many books on the market that can help you uncover the real "you." In fact, your career guidance counselor may recommend one of them to you or administer a personality profile test during one of your meetings. If you are the type of person who is receptive to such advice, great. These books and tests are amazingly accurate assessment tools and can be useful aids in helping you verbalize the values you consider important and the skills you truly enjoy. They will not, however, tell you what you don't already know. Many people respond to these books and tests in one of two ways: either they love them and consider them accurate barometers of their personalities because the books and tests pinpointed those aspects of their personalities already known to them, or they consider them to be faulty because they reached results contrary to what the reader or test taker knows about themselves.

Given that most people only believe in them when they tell them what they already know, the intrinsic value of these books and tests is questionable. When it comes to deciding whether to use them, the best advice is to follow your gut instinct. If you are a person who enjoys the scientific method and believes in the results, then use them. If you are more skeptical and question whether a book written by someone who has never met you can possibly pinpoint your personality profile accurately, then ignore them.

The truth is, whether you decide to use a book or not, you'll need to spend some time considering your core beliefs, values and interests before heading into the job market. Failure to do so will only result in a job search that focuses on what's available rather than what will make you happy. This can only lead to the disastrous results discussed in Chapters One through Three.

B. Identifying Your Interests

Spend some time (a large amount of time) just thinking about what you enjoy. Forget for a moment that you're looking for a job. This will only place artificial limitations on your thought process. What do you like to do in your free time? If you were employed prior to entering law school, what did you enjoy about these prior jobs? Remember, although you probably did not wholeheartedly love your prior job (after all, if you did then you wouldn't have gone to law school), there may have been aspects of it which intrigued you. Consider the classes you've taken in law school as well. Which ones do you enjoy? What is it about them that you find interesting? Is it the fact that there is a lot of writing involved? Or is it the fact that there is very little writing at all? Is it the complex statutory analysis you find intriguing? Were the mock negotiations or oral argument components the highlight of a particular class or classes? Spend some quality time considering not only what you like but *why* you like it.

Consider what you would do with yourself if you did not need to find a job. How would you spend your days? Although many people euphorically respond that they would spend their days lounging on a tropical beach, this is because they've never seriously considered the question. Law school (and the law) is an intellectual endeavor and the fact that you have

51

chosen it over the myriad of other professional tracks indicates that you have an intellectual curiosity that needs to be fed. If you think hard enough and seriously enough about the question, you would probably realize that you would become bored simply lying around doing nothing all day forever. So, once your "vacation" was over, what would you do?

Make a list of everything you enjoy. Don't worry if these things have nothing to do with "the practice of law." As stated earlier, everything either has a connection to the law or your ultimate happiness in some way. You'll worry about finding the connection later. For now, just concentrate on your interests. If you enjoy spending quality time with your dog, write that down. There is no objective list of appropriate interests for an attorney. Only you can make this determination. Ignoring something that is important to you simply because you believe it to be irrelevant to your job search will only cause you to be frustrated later on. We'll come back to your pooch later on in this chapter so you can see how crucial it was that you included him in your initial list of interests.

C. Focusing on Your Personal Values and Beliefs

Next, make a list of your values and beliefs. What is important to you? There is nothing worse than doing something for a living that contradicts your basic feelings regarding right and wrong. When considering these values and beliefs, start to think about the types of people you'd like to deal with on a daily basis. Who do you want to help? The little guy? Or the person/entity who may be the victim of others who attempt to take advantage of them? Do you want to be on the side of the government or the individual?

52

D. Creating the "Perfect Job"

After you've drawn up these lists, try to create what you consider "the perfect job." For the moment, don't worry if that job actually exists. Refer to both your "interests" and "values and beliefs" lists when considering what your perfect job would look like. What types of things would you be doing every day? Who would your clients be? When would you arrive at work? When would you go home? Where would you work – in the city, suburbs, or the country? How many people would you work with? Would you do a large variety of things or become an expert in a specific area? Would you take your dog to work with you or leave him home? What would you do when you came home from work in the evening? Be sure to number every element of your perfect job. You'll refer to these elements later when considering actual jobs.

Only now, once you've identified the elements of your perfect job, is it finally time for you to start looking for it.

Finding the Right Job for You

Since you now know what you want, the task now is to find *your* job rather than merely *a* job. This is what will differentiate you from most of your classmates. But what if your job isn't out there? After all, if you took the time to really think about your perfect job, you probably have a lengthy and specific list of elements your job will need to have. What is the likelihood that you'll be able to find an actual job that has all of them?

In actuality, pretty small. When searching for a job, it is important to remember that because you are a young attorney with little experience, the job with the short hours, corner office and dream clients most likely won't be available to you. Yet. However, your goal is not to get the perfect job *today*, it is to put you on a path where you'll be able to advance or transition into that perfect job a few years down the road. Remember, pigeonholing can work for you as well as against you. If you can land a job in an area of law you find interesting, and which is compatible with your values and beliefs, you'll be well on your way to a career that is emotionally satisfying. You'll also set yourself up for success because, as discussed in Chapter One, you can't help but succeed when you're doing what you love. Although there probably will be some significant "grunt work" that you as a junior attorney will have to do, as well as the stresses and aggravations that naturally come with a legal career, you'll be better equipped to withstand and overcome them because, in the end, you love what you do.

So while you may have listed 15 elements to your perfect job, your goal during your job search is to find the jobs right now which meet either the most or the most important of these elements rather than all of them. Some of the elements you listed are probably available to someone with more seniority. After all, more seniority usually equals more perks. If so, then you can feel confident that if you've chosen a field that meets your most important elements now, you'll only move closer to your perfect job as you gain experience in your chosen field. You'll know that you're moving in the right direction since you're on a path which leads to an even more satisfying job down the road.

Some elements of your perfect job may not be readily apparent in the jobs you are considering until you take the time to compare a particular job with your list. An example of this comes from Edgar F. Edgar repeatedly passed over a particular position because he considered the salary to be below his acceptable minimum. After he drew up his perfect job, however, he realized that this particular position matched the five most important attributes of his dream job – including the ability to bring his dog in to work with him. He hadn't included his pooch in his initial assessment of his dream job but added him in when he decided to shoot for the stars and describe his dream job in a perfect world. Little did he know how close he would actually come to his idea of professional perfection. On reflection, Edgar saw that he never would have realized how perfect this particular position was if he never had taken the time to create his "perfect job" list beforehand. Once he did, and once he was able to compare the position with his list, the salary issue became much less significant to him than it had been previously.

Edgar's experience shows the importance of keeping an open mind when considering your interests, values and beliefs, and your perfect job. Be careful not to limit yourself or to exclude something simply because you consider it to be unreasonable or "stupid." If you consider something to be important, then it most certainly is not stupid to you. Only when you truly take the time to analyze yourself first can you then develop the ability to identify the right job for you when it presents itself. Judging by all of the unhappy people out there (lawyers as well as non-lawyers), this skill is a learned one and one that few people have been able to master. So if it is important to you, remember to keep in mind such non-legal or "off the wall" interests as your pooch. You never know when one or more of them will be satisfied in a job you might otherwise gloss over. The right job for you is out there. However, you have to take the time to first identify the real "you" before you'll be able to see it clearly.

Making Sure That You Get the Job That You Want

A.   Identifying the Hidden Land Mines in the Job Negotiation Process

Once you've identified a particular job or area of the law that interests you, your next task is to make sure that you get it. Many people successfully negotiate the career identification process only to hit a landmine here, when they thought they were home free. You will be able to avoid a similar fate if you are able to see the landmines before you step on them. This section will help to improve your vision in this area.

Consider the following scenario (it is one that is played out far too often): You have concluded that product liability law is the area that most closely matches your interests. You have identified a firm that has a product liability law department and that represents the type of clients you'd like to represent and have managed to land yourself an interview. During the interview, things are going well; it seems likely that you will receive an offer. You are excited to be joining such a prestigious firm and they seem to be excited to have you join them. However, there is one problem: the product liability group does not currently have a position available. Not to worry, the interviewer says when she calls to make your formal offer, she has spoken to the head of the product liability group and he promises to send some product liability cases your way. Thus, although you will "officially" be joining the automotive litigation group, you will get plenty of product liability experience as well. This seems fair to you so you accept. It will only be a few years later, when you look back on that conversation, that you will realize that you stepped right on a landmine.

It may be hard to see the landmine when you initially step on it. After all, your firm was not lying when it promised to send some product liability cases your way. You did, in fact, receive some cases. However, as time went on, you received fewer and fewer such cases and, frankly, you were so busy with your automotive cases that you found that you just didn't have the time to spend on these additional ones which you soon viewed as a burden. While, at the time, you were relieved to be receiving fewer product liability cases, you now look back upon your decision with regret because you are now an automotive liability lawyer when you really wanted to be a product liability lawyer. So what happened?

What happened is that you were sweet talked during your interview into taking a job that promised much more than it could ever hope to deliver. No matter what the interviewer promised, there was no realistic chance that those product liability cases would ever be anything other than a burden to you – one that you would be happy to relieve yourself of at the first opportunity. Which at first blush seems odd, given that you truly enjoy product liability law. In order to understand this apparent oddity, it is necessary to first develop an understanding of how law firms manage associates.

B. The Dynamics of the Law Firm Partner-Associate Relationship

The larger the law firm, the more departmentalized it becomes. However, even small law firms are typically broken into practice groups. When associates join a firm, they join one of these groups and the partners in these groups assume the ultimate responsibility for their associates. While the entire partnership may officially be called upon to vote on whether a particular associate should advance or be given a raise, most of the partners from other departments generally defer to the judgment of the partners within the associate's group. After all, it is the partners within a particular associate's group who work with her on a daily basis and are in the best position to judge her performance.

Although this makes perfect sense, it can lead to unwelcome results (at least from the associate's perspective) when associates take on work outside of their assigned groups. Thus, returning to the previous example, even though you enjoy product liability law, you cannot afford to spend much time on these cases because your overall performance will be judged more on your work in the automotive group than anything you do for a product liability group partner. After a while, as you gain more experience, your workload within the automotive group will naturally increase, leaving you with less and less time to work on the product liability cases.

At the same time, as you gain experience you will be expected to handle cases which are more difficult and involve issues far more complex than the ones you worked on when you first started out. Being able to successfully handle these cases naturally requires you to become somewhat of a specialist in a particular area of the law. Since you cannot, given the time restraints, handle enough product liability cases to sufficiently train you as a specialist in this area, you will invariably start to feel uneasy handling them despite your initial attraction to this area of the law. You will naturally feel more comfortable handling the auto cases, even though you do not find auto cases particularly interesting, simply because you have become familiar with this area of the law. Given that your future at the firm rides on your ability to handle the auto cases you do not enjoy and not on the product liability cases you initially enjoyed but which now make you nervous, you cannot help but view the product liability cases as a burden and a potential hindrance to your future. All of which is a shame because above everything else, you really do enjoy product liability law much more than the auto cases. It is just that as you advance through a firm, it is not possible for you to satisfy your interest if it is nothing more than a side dish.

Too many law students focus on simply landing a job with a firm rather than landing a job in their department of choice within that firm. They're happy to accept whatever morsels are tossed at them if they so dare to specify the particular departments in which they have an interest, not realizing until it is too late that these morsels are nothing more than window dressing on an otherwise undesirable job that will leave them unhappy for years to come.

This is particularly unfortunate because, as the following section shows, it is the law student who typically holds the upper hand in job negotiations with a law firm. It is within the law student's power to dictate the specific job of his or her choice rather than meekly accept whatever is thrown their way. However, as a law student, you must act quickly on your advantage because the balance of power quickly shifts to the firm and then there is nothing you can do about it.

The Balance Of Power Between Law Student and Law Firm

Part of Chapter Two of this book focused on the law firm's decision-making process when it comes to hiring experienced attorneys as well as newly-minted grads. As you read in that section, newly-minted grads have a competitive advantage over experienced attorneys wishing to switch substantive areas of law because the salaries and training costs of the newly-minted grads are relatively fixed whereas these costs can vary widely with someone more experienced. This is true even in a down economy. Moreover, since it is assumed that students are essentially clueless when it comes to knowledge of substantive law in their practice area of choice, it makes little practical difference to a firm whether a particular student wants to join one department over another; the firm will pay the new associate the same approximate starting salary and expend similar training resources regardless. As a student, these factors give you bargaining leverage with your law firm of choice. You can use your leverage to negotiate a position in your practice area of choice. Failure to act on your advantage now, when you have the chance, will result in an opportunity lost forever since the balance of power quickly shifts to the firm once you've accepted your initial position out of law school.

Most students have a difficult time believing that they -- inexperienced, jobless and clueless -- can possibly hold the upper hand in negotiations with a prestigious and powerful law firm. But it's true. How is this possible? Consider the following:

You've spent the summer following your second year in law school as a summer associate with a prestigious firm. You've taken assignments from many different partners in many different departments and decided that the real estate department is the one you'd like to join. During your exit interview, you are asked which departments you enjoyed the most and you respond by singling out the real estate department. You further add that while you'd accept an offer from that department, you would not accept one from any other. Your interviewer is somewhat startled by this response but marks it down. A few months later, you receive an offer from the real estate department.

Why did you get an offer from your department of choice? Because, from the firm's perspective, it really doesn't matter which department you join. The firm is essentially going to pay you the same starting salary and spend the same amount of time training you regardless. The only important factor from the firm's perspective is that they like you and your work. If so, they want to give you an offer. If you're not convinced that this is the case, take a few moments to page through your NALP Directory, focusing on the percentage of summer associates who receive permanent job offers. You'll notice that most firms extend offers to 80-95% of their summer associates. Those who fail to receive offers are generally people who clashed personally with someone at the firm or whose work was substandard. If you're like most summer associates and do quality work while presenting yourself as someone others would want to work with, you stand an overwhelming chance of receiving an offer. And once your firm decides that you are someone who would fit in well, you can, to a large extent, dictate the department you join.

Of course, there is always the possibility that the real estate department doesn't have an opening for a newly-minted grad. If such is the case, then regardless of how much you liked the firm and the people, *you don't want to work there.* Accepting a job in a department that does work you do not enjoy will only result in your being unhappily pigeonholed for years to come. And, as stated earlier in this chapter, the possibility of having a few real estate files sent your way is likewise unattractive and will only result in a work scenario you'd be better off avoiding.

The power dynamic between firm and newly-minted grad discussed above is essentially the same when it comes to small firms or sole practitioners. Think of each of these smaller, more narrowly focused, firms as the equivalent of a large firm's various departments. Ask yourself whether the firm in question practices the type of law you wish to practice. If it does, great – regardless of the classes you took while in law school the balance of power is in your favor. If you can demonstrate to this firm that you possess the potential to improve, it will seek your services and you hold the upper hand in the ensuing employment negotiations. If, on the other hand, the firm is comprised of great people who primarily practice automotive liability law rather than your beloved real estate law, skip it and move on to the next opportunity even though the firm promises to send the few real estate files that come through its door your way.

As a general proposition, if a medium or large firm likes you well enough, it will work to create an opening in your department of choice. Smaller firms may not have as much flexibility but will still try to accommodate you if at all possible (but beware – if the firm doesn't appear to handle enough cases in the area of law you desire, be prepared to turn down any offers that come your way regardless of what the hiring attorney promises you. Don't be sweet-talked into taking a job that doesn't match your career interests). And remember, when it comes to small firms, no matter where you live there are undoubtedly many more of them around than there are medium and large firms. If one doesn't offer what you're looking for, keep searching. Eventually you'll find what you're looking for. Regardless of the size of the firm you're dealing with, don't worry about ruffling a few feathers by standing up for yourself and stating what it would take for you to accept an offer. Most firms will appreciate your honesty and ability to advocate for yourself (after all, if any employer is going to admire an employee who is willing to fight for what they want, it is going to be a law firm). And if a particular firm cannot, or will not, work to make available a position in your department of choice, then you don't want to work there anyway. You have nothing to lose, job-wise, and everything to gain by plainly stating your intentions to a potential employer. You have everything to lose, career-wise, if you sit back and allow your field of law to be chosen for you by a firm that otherwise will place you in a position which merely fills whatever need is most pressing at a particular moment.

None of this is to suggest, however, that law firms are desperate to offer employment to anyone, merely because they are a newly-minted law school graduate. People with poor grades or social skills will have a difficult time finding employment at any stage of their career and regardless of the state of the economy. Unless they have incredible connections, these people will never have any leverage over a law firm in the job seeking process (and even with those connections they will most likely be flushed out of most firms within a few years). While there may be books on the market which profess that *anyone*, regardless of their grades, can land a job *anywhere*, the truth is that it will always be more difficult for the people on the bottom end of the curve. Grades matter. However, given that most law students possess GPA's in the B range or better, they are the type of people law firms are looking to hire. They are the ones who, through impressive demonstrations of their work ethic and social skills, have the ability to impress firms enough to make them an offer. Once this is done, the power rests on the students' side of the bargaining table. At this point, it is up to you, the student, to use your leverage to your advantage or suffer the consequences for the rest of your career.

In the end, this opportunity, like all those that have come before it and which have been discussed in this book, is one that is entirely within your grasp. The choice to become a happy lawyer is yours and yours alone. Act now or you will be forever after asking questions later.

Chapter Five: Student Loans, the Economy, and Your Future

All of what has been covered thus far may be well and good, you might be saying to yourself right now, but what about my student loan debt, what about the terrible economy – don't these, unquestionably very real, concerns take precedence over my selfish desire for happiness? Shouldn't I take whatever's offered my way now, or accept the offer promising the highest starting salary and worry about professional fulfillment later? Given my debt and the current shaky state of things in the legal profession, isn't the bottom line when it comes to job-seeking, well, the bottom line? In a word, no.

<u>Your Student Loan Debt Cannot Dictate the Rest of Your Life</u>

Let's focus on student loan debt first since this is invariably first and foremost on the minds of most law students and young professionals. For many, soon after the euphoria over being admitted to law school dies down, anxiety over how to pay for it begins to take over. By the time graduation rolls along, law school debt for many is in the high five figures and, for some, in the six. Understandably, then, the question of just how all of this is going to be paid off dominates the conversation when it comes to job-seeking. Your mission is to make sure that it does not dominate you.

Of course, you cannot ignore the elephant in the room; you have loans that need to be paid off and you have a responsibility to ensure that you can meet your monthly obligation to do so. Realistically, just as you cannot sit on a beach and ignore them you cannot decide that your only employment will be on a pro bono basis while you hide from the collection agent. However, if you really want to take a job that you love, even though it pays less than a job you do not, you will probably find ways to meet your financial obligations anyway. In short, you may find that you can accept a lower salary than you might think and still pay off your student loans without hearing from the collection agent even once.

If this book has preached nothing else it's that your first job after law school is in many ways the most important one you will take as it determines the trajectory of your entire career. Given this, finding the *right* job must be your highest priority – higher than the amenities of the apartment you will rent, the car you will drive, the vacations you will take. For far too many young attorneys this is unfortunately not the case. Many celebrate law school graduation with the purchase of yet another substantial monthly obligation to go with their student loan payments – a new car. By resisting this temptation and driving the clunker you drove throughout law school (or by using public transportation if available), you suddenly will have an extra few hundred dollars each month to put toward your student loan payments. Consequently, your acceptable minimum starting salary just dropped a few thousand dollars per year as well, opening up potential employment opportunities that would have been shut off to you had you tried to one-up your friends by driving home with the shiniest new car you could find.

More money to put toward student loans (and which will likewise drive your acceptable minimum starting salary even lower) can come out of your apartment search as well. Do you really need to live on the top floor of the swankiest building in town? Definitely not, even though other young attorneys choose to spend their money this way. Can you take in a roommate? Can you choose to look for housing in a less pricey neighborhood? Can you find something within walking distance of public transportation? All of these things will save you money, facilitate your ability to meet your student loan obligations, and provide you with greater flexibility when it comes to your job search. If you apply this approach to all of your daily and monthly expenses you'll undoubtedly find many ways to reduce them, which will in turn provide more opportunities with regard to your job search. Even small savings can add up. Pack your lunch instead of buying it every day – it might eventually help you land the job of your dreams.

But what about those hearty souls (everybody knows a few) who claim that they're going to take the highest paying job available to them right out of law school solely to pay off their student loans, after which they'll be unshackled and free to take the job they always wanted? Isn't this a worthy model suitable for emulation? Aren't these folks taking a mature and well-reasoned approach to their finances? Once again, in a word, no.

While, in theory, this plan sounds great, in reality it breaks down in numerous ways. First, as you know by now, happiness leads to success and does not follow it. As such, there is little chance that the miserable, albeit highly-paid, associate will be able to continue earning her large salary long enough to allow her to pay off her student loans. Although she might be able to put a dent in her student loans for a few years or so, the shear drudgery of the work, and her attitude towards it, will doom her as the years pass and as those colleagues who truly enjoy the work she despises rise above her within her firm. Eventually, when the firm needs to tighten its belt, she'll be among the first to go, most likely well in advance of the date of her final student loan payment. At that point she'll be saddled with two burdens: the student debt she mistakenly thought she could erase and unwanted experience in a field of law she despises. From then on it's most likely one bad job after another for this unfortunate (and, very quickly, not-so-young anymore) attorney as she continues to chase high salaries while pigeonholing herself for the rest of her professional life.

Second, even if we assume that she does not lose her job, it's highly unlikely that she will be able to save enough as the years go on to pay off her loans in a reasonably short period of time. Passing up the shiny new car and the fabulous apartment is possible if you're otherwise getting up every morning and doing something that you truly love and which brings you deep satisfaction. Passing these things up as you trudge to work day after day, year after year, to a job you detest is much more difficult. When the money is the only reason for getting out of bed in the morning it's hard to pass up the treats money can buy as a means of compensating for deep-rooted dissatisfaction. Soon, as the baubles pile up, the end-date for the student loan payments moves further out to sea until eventually it disappears altogether over the dark, seemingly endless, horizon.

And finally, there's the issue of the nature of student loan debt itself and that of debt in general. Although right now it may seem impossible to believe, your student loan debt, sizable as it may be, will most likely not be the largest, and certainly will not be the only, monthly obligation you'll have to learn to deal with as you become a full-fledged professional adult. At some point (although hopefully, as noted above, not right out of law school), you may very well purchase a house, and then a car. You may also get married, have children and the corresponding expenses here will be significant as well. In short, you're going to have to learn to deal with debt and how to manage it; it is not a successful or practical strategy to imagine happiness only in a debt-free world. Regardless of your personal views on the nature of debt in modern America, it is a reality for almost everybody and you're going to have to learn how to achieve a certain comfort level with it. Those who prefer to run from their student loan debt by attempting to rid themselves of it as if it were a virus are doing themselves no favors and are taking a childish approach to an adult issue. They may seem like the most mature people in the room when discussing their plan but really, they are anything but. The key with all debt, and student loan debt is no different, lies in accepting its existence and managing it smartly. This not only can be done, it must be done. Moreover, it's a learned skill so no better time than the present to begin your education in this area of adulthood.

Understand the Economy and What it Means

Beyond student loan debt is the larger, more encompassing issue of the overall state of the economy (or, more specifically, the economy as it affects the legal profession). Making sense of this is vital to your success as a practicing attorney; avoid making snap judgments and then acting on them. You need to understand the implications of any sort of economic downturn (and, just as importantly, economic boom) and respond in ways that will

69

further your goal of professional satisfaction rather than hinder it. As an attorney, you're paid to be smart, to think deeply and to analyze facts and circumstances in detail. Make sure to do this in all aspects of your life.

More important than the causes of any particular recession (at least in terms of your job search), are the effects. Namely, you need to determine how a particular downturn implicates the nature and amount of jobs available to you. While no two recessions are exactly alike, they generally compel all businesses (and most law firms are, at their core, nothing else) to react in the same way. Specifically, economic downturns force all businesses to seek efficiencies wherever they can. Wherever they identify areas of waste, they will seek to reduce or eliminate them in order to maintain their bottom lines. What does this mean for you, the job seeker? Basically that whatever has been eliminated due to a recession is most likely not coming back once the economy picks up again. Why not? Because once a company, or a law firm, becomes more efficient it's not going to choose to revert to its less-efficient ways simply because it now has the capital once again to do so. Instead, it will seek to maintain the efficiency and reap the benefits of the greater profit margin.

This means that many of the specific jobs that were available prior to a recession simply are not coming back once things ease up. Not then, not ever. Due to the numerous workplace efficiencies created by the Internet, many firms adapted as times got tough over the past few years and discovered that much legal work no longer needs to be done "on site" anymore; it can be done just as well, and much more cheaply, in the firm's "satellite" offices located in India, South Korea, or even elsewhere in the United States in cities with lower standards of living and with more affordable office rental rates. As a result, the days of the big city mega-firm, with hundreds of junior lawyers reviewing documents in pricy cosmopolitan offices, are probably over. To be sure, there will still be mega-firms (in fact, many firms consolidate during down times, thus increasing the number of such creatures) in big cities, but many of their associates will be located in offices elsewhere. Rather than paying the enormous rental fees for ten floors of prime urban office space, the efficient large firm will from now on perhaps rent only two or three floors in the city and farm the rest of its work out to satellite offices across the country and the globe -- places where office space is cheaper, the cost of living is less, and where salaries are correspondingly more modest as well. Those graduates who believe that they'll simply "wait out" the current recession by taking whatever's available now, on the theory that more and varied work will become instantly available later, are misguided. To begin with, by taking a job they don't love they risk pigeonholing themselves for the rest of their careers. Worse, they're doing so under the false impression that their dream job will magically appear out of the blue and save them from a lifetime of drudgery.

So, if the jobs aren't coming back, what is a young law graduate to do? If the legal profession in the early part of the 21st century is indeed the functional equivalent of the steel industry of the 1970's, does this mean that all is lost? Hardly. There will always be a need for capable, hardworking attorneys and, contrary to the incessant cries within the popular media declaiming the unwanted glut of lawyers in America, many areas of the nation remain critically in need of legal services. It is your responsibility to figure out where jobs in your area of interest are available and to be prepared to do what it takes to get them. Sitting back, wistfully recalling the good ole' days when jobs literally fell out of the sky like raindrops and waiting for that fictional Eden to return, will get you nowhere. Simply stated, the rules that governed previous generations of law job seekers no longer apply in the digital age. You can either bemoan or accept this. The multitude of unhappy lawyers will choose the former, the happy ones the latter. Position yourself within the happy minority by accepting reality and vowing to be proactive in ways that will enable you to seek emotionally fulfilling work, the vagaries of the economy be damned.

How to do this? First, be prepared to go where the job of your dreams is, rather than wait for it to come to you. This means that you have to be geographically mobile. If there are jobs in the area of law that intrigues you in what you consider geographically undesirable places, you have to be willing to move to them nevertheless. This may very well require you to sit for additional state bar exams; if so, that's a small price to pay in order to achieve a lifetime of happiness and professional fulfillment. And who knows, you may discover that you enjoy life in a place you would never otherwise consider. Even if you don't, rest assured that you're not locked into a lifetime living in a hellhole. One of the upsides of the newly destabilized legal marketplace is that it's no longer considered unusual for attorneys to move from job to job several times before settling down for good. Don't forget that in those "good ole' days," young attorneys were expected to stay with their first job for the duration of their careers; moving from firm to firm was considered bad form and cast negative aspersions on those who did it. This only increased the pressure on law grads in those bygone days to make a perfect employment selection right out of the chute. If they made a mistake they were doomed to choose between a life of misery

72

in their firm or a reputation as a legal vagabond in the eyes of future employers. Embrace the newly-found freedom of young attorneys in the modern market; know that whatever job you accept now is most likely not going to be the last job you will ever have; understand that the path to your dream job will probably take you to several different places, working for different types of people, living and working in different environments; focus on what's important now: providing the bedrock for your career's journey.

Next, be sure to be singularly minded at this stage of your career. As a young attorney you cannot control everything within your work environment. That is, although there are many factors that contribute to your ultimate satisfaction (nature of the work, your camaraderie with your co-workers, geographic location, family concerns, etc.) you will most likely only be able to control one, at most two, at this point. What you choose now, however, will undoubtedly affect the rest of your life so be sure to choose wisely. You could focus only on salary but we've already discussed why and how this will ultimately doom you. You could also focus on the personality traits of your potential boss and co-workers and while these are ultimately important, they're not as important as working within an area of law that you find to be inherently satisfying. Remember, people, as well as legal jobs nowadays, come and go. Because of pigeonholing, however, your job choices are likely to narrow as you gain experience. While the best scenario would be for you to work for and with great people and doing work that's meaningful to you, achieving all of this right now might not be possible. Therefore, although it might be a difficult to do, be prepared to pass up the unfulfilling job with great folks for the more fulfilling one subject matter-wise with those you might not be as enamored with. Here again you might surprise yourself: you might discover that these folks aren't so bad after all. And if they are, not to worry – you'll most likely be picking up and leaving after a couple of years anyway. What you'll take with you is important experience in your field of interest which will give you more opportunities than you had as a newly-minted attorney. Now, with some important experience in your chosen, and meaningful, field, under your belt, you'll be able to look for another employment opportunity that is a better overall fit for you. As you move from one job to the next, you'll find that all of those other things that combine to determine your overall happiness will become increasingly available to you as you work your way up in your field of choice – which you will undoubtedly do if you're always doing something that engages and excites you. Those who chose people over subject matter right out of the chute may very well find themselves rethinking that decision a few years down the road when their beloved boss and co-workers desert them as they move on in their personal career journeys as well.

Finally, consider the possibility of a professional life that does not include private law firm practice. Traditionally, law grads were overwhelmingly funneled into law firms of one size or another. Although there were always a few who chose public interest work, the business world, government employment and the like, these were very much outliers within the field. Despite the shop-weary admonition that "one can do anything with a law degree," the reality was that for decades most worked in private law firms nevertheless. Today, however, this is becoming increasingly less true. According to a 2012 U.S. Law Week survey, 2011marked the first year in over three decades where the majority of law graduates with jobs accepted positions in places *other than* private firms. Moreover, the class of 2011 is clearly not an aberration; the percentage of employed law school graduates employed within private firms has been shrinking for a number of years. Here again, one can choose to see this glass as either half-empty or half-full. While this may very well mean that there are fewer law firm positions available than ever before (due to the outsourcing discussed earlier and other factors), it also means that the range of employment possibilities for law graduates is broader than at any time since the 1970's. At last, as the class of 2011 has demonstrated, that old admonition is finally true: you can do nearly anything with a law degree. Those who focus solely on law firms for employment can now count themselves within the minority of law school graduates. The modern graduate needs to look beyond this traditional feeding ground, to all of those other entities that would benefit from the advice and knowledge of a dedicated attorney. Even if those jobs would not constitute the technical "practice of law," they still have value and may very well open up a treasure trove of contacts and opportunities to you that a traditional law firm could never do.

The 21st century lawyer is, in many ways, flying blind. Many of the old rules no longer apply and the new ones have not yet been established. In such an atmosphere, stress and anxiety are a given as successes and mistakes oftentimes cannot be measured until years later, when the implications become more apparent. However, with the tossing off of the rules of the old establishment comes excitement and opportunity as well. Embrace the new; embrace the different; embrace the path not taken. Focus on what matters – doing something that you love, something that brings meaning and satisfaction to your life. The path will undoubtedly be rocky and hazardous at times but eventually you'll reach the sandy shore. So long as you're always headed in the right direction, you can't avoid it.

APPENDIX:

RESOURCES

There are numerous on-line and print resources to aid the law student or young lawyer seeking information on "what it's really like" to practice in various legal settings. What follows is a sampling of such material.

LIFE IN LARGE FIRMS

Mary A. McLaughlin, *Beyond the Caricature*, 52 Vand. L. Rev. 1003 (1999).
Describes the benefits and challenges of practicing in a large firm, told from a large firm advocate's point of view.

James Regan, *How About a Firm Where People Actually Want to Work*, 69 Fordham L. Rev. 2693 (2001).
Describes the nature of large firms and suggests methods for improvement. Tells what young lawyers should look for and look out for when choosing to work for a large firm. Discusses the roots of large firm job dissatisfaction.

A. Benjamin Archibald, *The False Dilemma*, 47 Boston Bar Journal 16 (Oct. 2003).
Provides statistics in an attempt to dispel some myths associated with large firm life.

Gary Munneke, *Opportunities in Law Careers*, 25-26, (rev. ed., VGM Career Books, 2001).
Brief insight into the organization of a large firm. Describes the evolving role of partners and senior associates in a large firm.

Patrick J. Schiltz, *On Being a Happy, Healthy, and Ethical Member of an Unhappy, Unhealthy, and Unethical Profession*, 52 Vand. L. Rev. 871 (1999).

Discusses the pros and cons of large firm life. Emphasizes the benefits of choosing small firm life instead.

Harvard Law School, Student Services, *Large Law Firms*, http://www.law.harvard.edu/students/slc/largelawfirm.php
Provides basic statistics, regional firm locations, other key websites and practice areas. Discusses working conditions in various firms as well.

New York Lawyer, *Large Firm Life: No Dodging the Draft*, http://www.nylawyer.com/news/02/08/080902d.html
Tells of beginning professional life in a large firm as a junior associate. Highlights the unpleasant tasks that come with it such as writing, revising, and research.

Dallas Business Journal, *Minorities Lagging at Big Law Firms*, http://www.bizjournals.com/dallas/stories/2003/11/10/story1.html
Provides statistics of women and minorities in large firms.

SMALL FIRMS

Lisa L. Abrams, *The Official Guide to Legal Specialties*, 389-409, (Harcourt Legal & Professional Publications, 2000).
Gives general description of the life of a small firm attorney. Discusses where they work, who their clients are, what types of cases they work on, as well as their daily activities. Also includes a discussion on what small firm attorneys find rewarding. Discusses important training and skills required of a small firm attorney. Includes a discussion of classes and law school experiences recommended for those aspiring to become small firm attorneys.

Carroll Seron, *The Business of Practicing Law*, (Temple University Press, 1996).
Portrait of the dilemmas and work lives of solo and small firm attorneys. Focuses on the typical work day of these attorneys as well as the range of clients available to them. Provides advice on how to choose a region in which to start a small or solo practice.

Donna M. Killoughey, *Breaking Traditions: Work Alternatives for Lawyers*, 117-124, (American Bar Association, 1993).
Describes the benefits of working in a small firm. Provides tips on how to balance one's professional and personal life.

Karen L. Pascale, *Small* Wonders, 19 Delaware Lawyer 17 (Spring 2001).
Personal lessons and advice from small firm lawyers and solo practitioners.

Donna Gerson, *Choosing Small, Choosing Smart*, (NALP, 2001).
Tells why young attorneys would enjoy small firms. Provides detailed description of the anatomy of a small firm. Describes how to get hired, be successful, and advance.

Gary Munneke, *Opportunities in Law Careers*, 21-23, (rev. ed., VGM Career Books, 2001).
Describes the freedoms that small firm lawyers enjoy relative to large firm lawyers. Points out some of the advantages and disadvantages of working in a small firm, including the potential financial constraints that may burden a small firm

Lawyers Weekly, *Small Law Firms Prove to be Big Source of Jobs*,
http://www.lawyersweeklyjobs.com/smallfirms.htm
Points out the advantages to working for a small firm over a large firm. Concludes that small firms are offering more job opportunities than ever before, and may offer superior work experience.

Patrick J. Schiltz, *On Being a Happy, Healthy, and Ethical Member of an Unhappy, Unhealthy, and Unethical Profession*, 52 Vand. L. Rev. 871 (1999).
Discusses the pros and cons of large firm life. Emphasizes the benefits of choosing small firm life instead.

Philip C. Williams, *From Metropolis to Mayberry*, (American Bar Association, 1996).
Gives accounts of those making the change from large firm life to small firms or solo practices. Contrasts the differences in practice and lifestyle.

SOLO PRACTITIONER

Lisa L. Abrams, *The Official Guide to Legal Specialties*, 389-409, (Harcourt Legal & Professional Publications, 2000).
Gives a general description of the life of a solo practitioner. . Discusses where they work, who their clients are, what types of cases they work on, as

well as their daily activities. Also includes a discussion on what solo practitioners find rewarding. Discusses important training and skills required of a solo practitioner. Includes a discussion of classes and law school experiences recommended for those aspiring to become solo practitioners.

Carroll Seron, *The Business of Practicing Law*, (Temple University Press, 1996).
Portrait of the dilemmas and work lives of solo and small firm attorneys. Focuses on the typical work day of these attorneys as well as the range of clients available to them. Provides advice on how to choose a region in which to start a small or solo practice.

Donna M. Killoughey, *Breaking Traditions: Work Alternatives for Lawyers*, 117-124, (American Bar Association, 1993).
Focuses on the concerns of solo practitioners as well as coping mechanisms.

Columbus Business First, *Solo Practice's Many Demands Include Self Motivation*, http://columbus.bizjournals.com/columbus/stories/2003/12/15/focus4.html
Tells of the advantages of the solo practitioner lifestyle.

Karen L. Pascale, *Small Wonders*, 19 Delaware Lawyer 17 (Spring 2001).
Personal lessons and advice from small firm lawyers and solo practitioners.

Gary Munneke, *Opportunities in Law Careers*, 21-23, (rev. ed., VGM Career Books, 2001).
Describes the freedoms that solo practitioners enjoy relative to large and small firm lawyers. Points out some of the advantages and disadvantages of working in a solo practice, including the potentially burdensome financial constraints.

Jeremy Smith, *Solo and Small Firm Practitioners Committee: Hints for Solo Practitioners*
32 American Bar Association Brief 10 (Spring 2003).
Discusses the wide array of pros and cons associated with life as a solo practitioner.

Heidi McNeil Staudenmaier, *Changing Jobs*, 200-205, (3d ed., American Bar Association, 1999).

Details the obstacles and fears to be overcome when one starts up a solo practice. Provides the author's tips for success.

American Bar Association, GP-Solo,
http://www.abanet.org/genpractice/Solo/home.html
Newsletter published by the ABA that discusses issues faced by small and solo practices.

Philip C. Williams, *From Metropolis to Mayberry*, (American Bar Association, 1996).
Gives accounts of those making the change from large firm life to small firms or solo practices. Contrasts the differences in practice and lifestyle.

A. Eduardo Balarezo, *From Park Avenue to Fifth Street, the Making of a Solo Practitioner*, American Bar Association, Criminal Justice Brief 13 (Winter 2003).
Discusses how to being and sustain a solo practice. Provides examples of the benefits and burdens associated with a solo practice.

Margaret Graham Tebo, *Battling The Solo Stigma*, 90 ABA J. 31 (February 2004). Discusses ways to overcome clients' perception that only a larger firm can properly handle their legal matters.

GOVERNMENT LAWYER

Stacy M. DeBroff, Jill P. Martyn & Alexa Shabecoff, *Serving the Public: A Job Search Guide, 14th ed.*, (Harvard Law School, 2003).
Lists numerous types of public service careers. Provides insight to dispel many common myths about public service. Includes personal narratives of particular public service careers.

Richard L. Hermann, Linda P. Sutherland & Jeanette J. Sobajian, *Federal Law-Related Careers Directory, 3d. ed.*, (Federal Reporters Inc., 1994).
Provides information geared towards understand the hiring process, the types of law related positions available in the federal government, and how to fill out federal application forms.

Lisa L. Abrams, *The Official Guide to Legal Specialties*, 191-210, (Harcourt Legal & Professional Publications, 2000).
Gives a general description of the life of a government lawyer. Discusses where they work, who their clients are, what types of cases they work on, as well as their daily activities. Also includes a discussion on what government lawyers find rewarding. Discusses important training and skills required of a government lawyer. Includes a discussion of classes and law school experiences recommended for those aspiring to work in the government.

Cornell W. Clayton, *Government Lawyers*, (University Press of Kansas, 1995).
Provides a listing and thorough description of various governmental legal practice areas. Includes information on careers in politics, judgeships and independent agencies. Discusses the ethical concerns faced by government lawyers.

U.S. Department of Justice, Do Your Legal Career, Justice: Opportunities for Entry-Level Attorneys and Law Students at the U.S. Department of Justice, (U.S. Department of Justice, 2000).
Gives listing of many jobs within the Department of Justice and their descriptions. Discusses what legal experience is needed, and what legal knowledge can be gained.

Gary Munneke, *Opportunities in Law Careers*, 34-41, (rev. ed., VGM Career Books, 2001).
Provides insight into a diverse range of government jobs such as federal or state attorneys general, and local district attorney. Also gives information on careers in the military, judicial administration, political administration, and politics. Points out some of the advantages to being a government lawyer.

American Bar Association, Law Students Division, *Now Hiring: Government Jobs for Lawyers*, (ABA, 1997).
Details many career options for lawyers interested in government careers.

Donna M. Killoughey, *Breaking Traditions: Work Alternatives for Lawyers*, 203-208, (American Bar Association, 1993).
Gives information on what to consider before going into government work. Provides a glimpse into the daily lives of government lawyers

McGeorge School of Law, Career Services, *Legal Careers in Government*, http://www.mcgeorge.edu/career_services/information_for_current_studen ts_and_alumni/legal_careers_in_government.htm
Provides information on the range of jobs available to a government lawyer. Discusses the positives and negatives of a career in the government.

Mike Davidson, *Confessions of a Convert*, 8 Nevada Lawyer 30 (Aug. 2000).
Personal observations from the perspective of someone entering the government from a private practice. Compares and contrasts the two types of work.

Heidi McNeil Staudenmaier, *Changing Jobs*, 213-253, (3d ed., American Bar Association, 1999).
Provides information on federal agencies, judgeships, and judicial administration positions. Outlines the skills required for different positions as well as how one may attempt to gain entrance into a particular governmental field.

CRIMINAL LAWYER

Lisa L. Abrams, *The Official Guide to Legal Specialties*, (Harcourt Legal & Professional Publications, 2000), pp. 109-131.
Gives a general description of the life of a criminal lawyer. Discusses where they work, who their clients are, what types of cases they work on, as well as their daily activities. Also includes a discussion on what criminal lawyers find rewarding. Discusses important training and skills required of a criminal lawyer. Includes a discussion of classes and law school experiences recommended for those aspiring to become criminal attorneys.

Seymour Wishman, *Confessions of a Criminal Lawyer*, (Times Books, 1981).
Provides a detailed account of each step of a criminal trial. Includes chapters on daily life, war stories, and conflicts that criminal lawyers face.

Gary Delsohn, *The Prosecutors*, (Penguin Group Inc., 2003).
One Journalist's account of a year in the life of the District Attorneys Office.

Bernard Asbell, *What Lawyers Really Do,* (Peter H. Wyden, Inc., 1970), pp. 62-81.
Although over three decades old, this remains an accurate and concise account of what at least one particular criminal defense lawyer faced in her life and work.

IN-HOUSE COUNSEL

Clifford R. Ennico, *Business Lawyers Handbook,* PG, (Clark Boardman Callaghan, 1992).
Discusses what a business lawyer (including an in-house lawyer) needs to know in order to succeed. Provides a "how to" guide to functioning in the business world, including: how to counsel clients, manage transactions, negotiate, and remain organized.

Lee Hugh Goodman, *The Case of Mistaken Identity*, 46 Federal Lawyer 42 (April 1997).
Discusses the difference between in-house lawyers and general practice lawyers. Focuses on the corporate concerns that influence the legal practice of an in-house lawyer.

Bernard Asbell, *What Lawyers Really Do,* (Peter H. Wyden, Inc., 1970), pp. 45-61.
Although over three decades old, this remains an accurate and concise account of one particular in-house attorney's professional life.

American Lawyer Media, Law.com, *In-House Counsel Quality of Live Survey 2003*, http://www.law.com/jsp/article.jsp?id=1069170407667
Provides stats regarding quality of life of in-house attorneys.

Heidi McNeil Staudenmaier, *Changing Jobs*, (3d ed., American Bar Association, 1999), pp. 206-212.
Provides tips on how to find and secure in-house positions.

NON-PRACTICING LAWYER

Deborah Aaron, *What Can You Do with a Law Degree*, 113-127, 167-244, apps. 4-5, (4th ed., Niche Press, 1999).
Discusses techniques for researching alternative careers. Tells how to job hunt, improve resume, and market yourself once you've decided to pursue an alternative career. Provides job options and job descriptions for selected alternative areas of practice.

Federal Reports, Inc., *JD Preferred: Legal Career Alternatives*, (Federal Reports, Inc., 1995). Gives career guidance, job descriptions, and pay scales in many alternative careers including academic administration and alternate dispute resolution.

Donna M. Killoughey, *Breaking Traditions: Work Alternatives for Lawyers*, 215-240, (American Bar Association, 1993).
Discusses several alternative career employment options as well as the factors an attorney should evaluate before transitioning into a non-traditional career

Heidi McNeil Staudenmaier, *Changing Jobs*, 298-307, (3d ed., American Bar Association, 1999).
Details the skills needed in non-traditional careers and techniques used to secure such a position.

Gary Munneke, *Opportunities in Law Careers*, 51-58, (rev. ed., VGM Career Books, 2001).
Provides brief description of some alternative careers, such as, administration and management, money management, planning and organization, insurance, administration of justice, real estate, legislation, communications, and education. Lists skills that may be called upon in these areas.

University of North Carolina Law School, Career Services, *Alternative and Non-Traditional Careers*,
http://www.law.unc.edu/career/cdplib/alternative.html
Provides numerous sources for researching alternative careers.